First Kiss

From The Initial Kiss To A Long Lasting And Enduring Love A Change Of Heart: Love Transformation Through A First Kiss

(Indulge And Experience Profound Joy At This Moment)

Jamison Lowery

"Mama wants to know if you want more eggs, Miss Lancaster."

At her lodging, Lucy was enjoying her breakfast at the inn. There were just two guests, and she hadn't seen the other one show up yet. Lucy's owner, whom the people in the small town called "Miss Hildie," was determined to put on some weight for her visit, believing that Lucy was far too thin.

"Oh no, Sylvie, I'm so sorry, but I really appreciate it." With a bowl full of fried potatoes in hand, Miss Hildie emerged from the kitchen just after Sylvie turned back toward it. Lucy grabbed her stomach and laughed when she saw her. "I really couldn't eat one more bite, ma'am."

"You don't eat, which is why you're as thin as a rail."

For breakfast this morning, Lucy had eaten more than she usually would in a whole day. She would detest meeting the person Miss Hildie thought had a good appetite.

"I'm really full, but it was great." I must depart for Salt Cedar Ranch.

"Oh! I was aware that you were in the area to handle some legal business. I had no idea it was for those adorable children. Kayla, how are you doing? She hasn't been in town in months, I swear.

"She seemed to be doing well. She informed me that her opportunities to leave the ranch are few. It seems like she puts in a lot of work.

"What a miserable child, losing both her parents when she was just twenty-one years old. Then Tuck Stevenson, the old tomcat, started closing in on them. I have no idea how she manages to accomplish it all.

It does appear to be a lot. At least she has her brother.

Hildie chuckled. "Gavin Walker isn't a businessman, but he's the best at training horses and wooing girls. However, you had better watch your drawers, my dear, since that boy only needs to glance at them on a gorgeous girl before they fall.

The mention of Gavin Walker "getting into her drawers" made Lucy's cheeks turn red. Miss Hildie might have her word that it would never happen. It wasn't as though she didn't think he was handsome. His dark brown hair stood out in small curls beneath the felt cowboy hat, and his hazel eyes looked green when he was passionate about his property and brown when he was irritated. It would take blindness to miss these details. Yes, she had noticed all of that in addition to the way his Wranglers fit so tightly on his long legs and the way his t-shirt's short sleeves pulled across his biceps that they appeared to be about to tear. She had observed and valued everything just like a beautiful artwork. It was only meant to be observed; never touched. Being in contact with it would trigger several alerts, and Lucy was too astute for that.

"Don't worry," she said to the senior citizen. "My drawers are cinched tight."

Hildie laughed heartily at that and flung back her head. After thanking her once more for breakfast, Lucy headed out to pick up her rental car. Just past seven in the morning. Someone like Kayla, she was sure, had to be awake by now. She couldn't wait to visit the disputed land and take some photos. Her phone rang, like if it knew what was on her thoughts. She got a call from Kayla Walker.

"Hi, Kayla. I was about to give you a call.

"Lucy, good morning. I wanted to inform you that Gavin, my horse, is already out in the pasture and that my horse is foaling this morning. Until she does, I won't be able to leave her and go take pictures with you outside.

"Oh, I see. Well, I don't mind going out on my own if you just give me the directions.

"Are you certain? I attempted to contact Gavin to ask whether he could meet you there, but he occasionally experiences service issues.

"Oh no!" Lucy remarked, gagging at the idea. She said, "I mean, don't bother him," after realizing how that sounded. I am able to handle.

Kayla consented and texted Lucy the location of the land after they had hung up. She would have to navigate some winding dirt roads to get there, but she had been wise enough to rent a four-wheel-drive car just for this kind of situation. They all assumed Lucy was more "city" than she actually was.

With the certainty that she wouldn't have to meet Gavin today, she happily made her way to the ranch. There were no signs of life when she drove the six miles to the ranch and passed the home and stables. She let out one last sigh of relief because she had been afraid she might run into him. After passing the turn-out pens, she did as Kayla had instructed and turned right. She went by another small house about a mile after making the first turn. It had a red door and red trim, and the front porch was framed by charming small yellow daisies. The house was brown. Lucy pondered whether the enormous red vehicle that was parked in front belonged to Gavin. She concluded that the likelihood was not. She had a photo of him with a log home and an old beat-up truck.

As instructed by Kayla, she turned at the gulch for her next turn. As far as she could recall, the instructions stopped there. She pulled her phone out of her purse. At that moment, the Land Rover encountered an uneven patch of road. Lucy leaned out and grabbed the wheel with both hands right away. She overcorrected by mistake when she did. The next several seconds felt like they were moving slowly. The car's tires skidded off the side of the road as she withdrew to the right. She pulled too quickly to the left when she felt it slide. That's when the little four-wheel-drive flipped over on its side, skidded for ten feet or so before coming to a sideways stop in a large hole at the side of the road.

For a brief while, Lucy sat there, attempting to orient herself and make sure everything was well. She reached for her seatbelt when she got her breath and saw that she didn't appear to have any broken bones or open wounds. Her left side was so tightly crushed by the SUV's side that her seat was shoved into the console. Her hand was stuck between them, preventing her from unbuckling the belt. With her seatbelt on, she was unable to reach the other door as the car rested on top of hers.

"Slow down! Alright, Lucy, relax. Inhale deeply and focus your thoughts. You're capable of handling this. Tears were gathering in the corners of her eyes, and she could feel their searing sting. "Quit it! Lucy, you're a mature woman. Not a single tear.

"Hey!" Is there anyone inside? She was taken aback by the rich, baritone voice.

Indeed! Here I am. My seatbelt won't come undone.

"Are you alright?"

Yes, that seems likely. Simply put, I'm stuck.

"Okay, give it a moment."

It was then that she understood, terrifying herself, that she had heard the voice before. That was Gavin Walker's. Oh, that's awesome! This is all he needed to conclude that she was utterly incompetent.

After a minute or so, she noticed his shadow obstructing the sunlight coming in through the window. The passenger door would not budge when he attempted to pull it open.

He gave the command, "Put your arms over your face and turn your head away from me."

After following his instructions, she would have leaped approximately a foot if she hadn't been securely restrained. He struck the window's corner with an object, shattering the glass. He tapped the remaining glass carefully until there was nothing but a hole. Then she heard him lean through the window to peer inside, and she heard the metal creak and groan beneath his weight. A broad smile spread across his face as soon as he spotted her. She might have blacked his other eye if she could have reached him.

"I think this is better than anything I've ever seen,"

"Would you mind getting me out of here when you're done making fun of me?"

He smiled once again, but happily he kept his mouth shut. Stretching his long arms down to where she sat, he laid on his tummy in the window. With a knife in one hand, he used the other to remove the seatbelt from her chest, sending shivers down her spine with his fingers.

Lucy, get your act together! This arrogant cowboy would have no interest in knowing that he made any sort of impression on you. Put it away!

He cut the seatbelt with the knife. She was set free as the blade effortlessly cut through it like butter. She inhaled deeply before murmuring, "Thank you."

Once more, he grinned at her. You're probably lucky that the airbag didn't go off. I'm going to descend. Do you really believe you can get up and get out?

"Yes, I believe so," she replied, observing her precise sitting position.

"All right, climb as high as you can; I'll pull you out the rest of the way."

Though she was forced to eat the armadillo that had been left on the road for a week, she preferred not to. She pushed herself up and wiggled her legs out under the steering wheel. Suddenly, he reached under her arms and pulled her out of the window when she had her body about halfway out. Her entire body was tingling, and it didn't seem to need any effort on his side. Once upright, she caressed her blouse and idly stroked her lengthy, wavy ponytail with her fingers.

Naturally, Boatrica won't punish students for arriving late for the opening ceremony, and Miyeon doesn't think the prior newbie had three sparks since she offended people right away and was only Draco's harbinger. Since it's the opening ceremony in the end, being late is not ideal.

Boatrica was practically understanding and cheerful despite her and Draco's tardiness, readily making fun of all her peers.

reveal who she is.

Don't wait around; perhaps this appeal is too strong.

A sob could be heard below after Boatrica's introduction.

The proverb "the gentleman's revenge for ten years" is quite genuine; the majority of them were taken aback. A few people even tried to deceive

Miyeoninto liking Lucius Malfoy, and as a result, she narrowed her eyes. She's the manager, so it's not too late; I can figure things out slowly.

Being extremely moral on the first day of the magical world is not hazardous.

While waiting for the opening ceremony to conclude—the time was not early—Miyeon returned to her apartment by herself, leaving her luggage behind and just foolishly laying on the bed.

It is referred to as a distorted Naamah when one thinks about parents, small disarray, and the belief that this body is the original owner. Name

She distinctly recalled that this individual had not been named in the original tale, and that there had not even been any indication of the kind of Hogwarts that the new management would leave behind.

Was Naamah initially ineligible for this position? Is it all a result of her transition? Does that mean that this prospective female pervert has changed too, or not?

As per the initial indication, both Lucius and the red shaman survived, thus naturally, the sage would not be lost; she took the place of Lucius's murderous wife; the original NaamahNaamah only had There are two possible outcomes: joining the opposing side in the conflict and being the most unknown sacrifice; or just being lucky enough to survive; however, the latter is a perversion and is said to be unlikely to give Lucius any hope at all, since he would ultimately have to spend the rest of his life alone.

Thus, consider how miserable that wicked woman is as well. For a guy is wasteful in order to have a happy life.

When Miyeon considered this, some consensus started to emerge despite the original Naamah.

Yes, that woman could be a little twisted, but to put it plainly, those are the eyes of death. Given that this is an example, it makes sense why she indicated that the eyes of death did not end well.

I'm not sure how, but when she recollects her family honoring her and cooking rice porridge with her until midnight when she first fell in love, her inner voice was urging her to hold off.

A guy has the right to change his mind and bide his time for the perennial tree to fall. Don't think about it, don't think about it, reconsider, or else you'll be mistaken for the rest of your life.

Miyeon chuckled aloud, thinking of this area.

She chuckles, "Maybe in this kind of situation, should she say that she likes to be too strong and will suffer for fun, or that her nerves have become sufficiently strong from reading?"

Maybe both of these points have been lost. Indeed, she likely believes that she will have the opportunity to come back.

Many female protagonists have had their lives brutally cut short in order to return to the original setting, whether it be from a horrific prior life or something like an automobile accident. miserable, with no relationship to the original world

However, she is not; she does not recall dying herself. She even believed that her parents had this thought of her sister. Could all of these be the same kind of king and dream? One day, she said, she woke up from a sleep and discovered that she was still on the plane. She then got off the plane and saw the happy faces of her parents, continuing to lie around here and there?

Miyeon thought, perhaps I was too tired today, and she fell asleep quickly. Once more, waiting for her is a crazy dream.

------oOo-----Rumors of a wild dream scenario in Chapter 5

In the dream, Miyeon saw a group of people—either known or unknown—passing by on their own. She tried to grab onto them, but her own hand instantly passed through their upper body. Disregarding her even more, it abruptly vanished from her field of vision without showing any signs of halting.

The Romance Goes On

Nana Lily jolts me from 1944 with, "I'm just going to the shops to get us some lunch."

Alright, My voice sounds strained as I yell, overcome with guilt at almost being caught reading these love letters. The glass inserts rattle as the front door slams shut.

I get up and extend. If these letters were Grammy's secrets, maybe I shouldn't be reading them. I plan to continue working as I sit down, but the letters are calling to me. I am powerless to resist.

I exhale, then carry the box, picture, and letters I've read to my bed. I drop to the ground and rest my back on the bed's leg. Although sleeping on the duvet might be more comfortable, it would be uncomfortable to read a love letter to Grammy while lying on my great-grandparents' bed.

I lay everything out on the floor next to me so I can see the picture while I read, and then I reach in to get the next letter. The date on it is September 10, 1944.

My sweetheart English Rose, your shrewdness and fast thinking continue to amaze me. How fortunate it was that the Major's vehicle broke down en route to his meeting in London, and how astute you were to volunteer to give him a lift back. Naturally, curfew meant that you had to remain overnight.

We had dinner in the neighborhood pub, which was a great treat. You were brave to meet my friends at the bar afterwards. The most memorable part, though, was when we were about to return to the barracks. The only time we spent the entire evening together was for that minute or two when I pulled you back behind the steps.

Your blue eyes captivated me, and your lips formed a small smile that appears when you're thinking positive ideas. Even though I knew better, I couldn't help myself. I reached down and put my lips to yours. I just wanted to steal a quick kiss, but I was gone when you put your arms around me and kissed me again.

I slid my hands over the curves of your back, my heart racing so fast I thought I might have a heart attack.

I'm sorry, but I felt like embracing you and bringing you upstairs. Luckily, the bartender cut us off. I apologize if I embarrassed you in any way; as I said my goodbyes, your cheeks turned red.

I'm not sorry, even though I should be, for taking advantage of you. The kiss left a lasting impression.

I have just one month left before my next trip to London.

Until then, Marlon, yours.

Whoa, it seems like Grammy kissed a different man, and it was a really passionate and heated kiss.

The idea is making my head spin. Grammy was getting old by the time I started thinking about kissing boys. She was elderly, but she was still gorgeous and it was obvious that she had been quite the sight in her younger years. It was shocking to discover that she had kissed a GI in a dimly lit hallway.

My hand is going for the next letter, an undated one, even as these ideas race through my mind.

My sweetheart English Rose,

I hope you receive this before my planned leave of absence and that you don't have to wait at the station wondering whether I've abandoned you. Although he is unsure if he will be able to visit your office this week, my friend assures me that he will forward it to someone who can deliver it to you.

Something is moving us. For obvious reasons, I can't write you where, but whoever delivers this should be able to tell you roughly where it is.

I won't be able to visit London, but my leave date remains the same. I'll write as soon as I can.

Marlon, you

Marlon's worry over the error shows through in the letter. It could not have been easy to organize to catch up and then had to make last-minute planned changes when there was a war going on. It wasn't like he could send a little text, really.

There are four more letters in the packet to read, so I'm very confident they got together again. I turned to the next one, November 28, 1944, and continued reading.

My lovely and astute Rose

Since we have been working long shifts, I haven't had time to write. You have to consider me to be a cad, as you English people say. You probably think that because I achieved what I desired, I've abandoned you. Maybe I haven't gotten what I want yet, but I'm not that kind of man. That is a jest.

Sweetheart Rose, When you finally showed up in Portsmouth, I was blown away. My eyes were seeing things my brain was not able to grasp, and all I wanted to do was stand there and take it all in.

Thankfully, you don't just have the looks—you also have the brains—and you grabbed my arm to show me where the tea house was. You filled in the silence as I stood there silently, amazed at my good fortune.

I volunteered to walk you back to the army base, where guests usually stay, as the sun started to drop. Then you shocked me by telling me that the army believed you were staying with relatives and that I had to bring you back to my accommodations or else you would have to spend the night on the streets.

You weren't joking, despite what I assumed. I thought I would burst into tears of excitement when you told me you loved me and that life was too uncertain to put things off. That was, without a doubt, the greatest night of my life.

I went to see my commanding officer today and requested permission to get married to you because only then will I be able to have what I really want, which is a future together.

I'm hoping to get permission to ask you the question I've been dying to ask before I go on Christmas break.

Marlon, your ever-loving

I'm hooked with Grammy Rose's letters right now. She had an extramarital affair with a US soldier. I'm not a prude, and I think well of her, but in the past...I suppose a lot of girls were doing it and going about their lives as if tomorrow never came. And a ton of them were also falling for GIs. As a school project, I once completed a family tree and came across almost 6,000 marriages between British women and American soldiers. Go Grammy! Still!

Of course! Here are some further suggestions to carry on with your quest for personal development and betterment:

Accept discomfort: Make it a habit to push yourself outside your comfort zone. Adopting a new approach, accepting a difficult assignment, or confronting a fear—embracing discomfort can result in increased potential and personal development.

Engage in self-compassion: Be kind, understanding, and forgiving to yourself. Acknowledge that errors are inevitable because you are a human. You may overcome disappointments and keep a great relationship with yourself by practicing self-compassion.

Develop your emotional intelligence and Increase your emotional intelligence by learning to recognize and understand both your own and other people's feelings. Making wiser judgments, handling disagreements, and navigating relationships are all aided by this ability.

Take regular pauses to relax: Make rest and relaxation a priority when practicing self-care. Give yourself permission to rest and recover; it will improve your output, your creativity, and your general health.

Encourage a growth mentality by taking on an attitude that welcomes difficulties, views setbacks as teaching moments, and has faith in your own ability to improve. Adopting a growth mindset makes it possible to make improvements over time.

Examine your interests and passions: Allocate time for pursuits and interests that make you happy and fulfilled. In addition to being enjoyable, participating in activities you're passionate about promotes self-expression and self-discovery.

Show appreciation for what you have: Develop an attitude of thankfulness by recognizing and appreciating your life's blessings on a daily basis. This exercise helps you focus on your successes and encourages an optimistic outlook.

Establish appropriate limits in both your personal and professional lives. Establish clear boundaries and prioritize your needs in order to keep a healthy balance and safeguard your wellbeing.

Gain efficient time management skills: By mastering efficient time management strategies, you may increase your output and efficiency. Set priorities for your job, get rid of distractions, and make a plan that will allow you to work with intention and attention.

Develop resiliency: By practicing coping strategies, keeping an optimistic mindset, and taking lessons from prior setbacks, one can become more resilient. You can overcome obstacles, overcome hardship, and preserve your mental and emotional health by being resilient.

Develop your active listening abilities to help you communicate more effectively. Pay close attention to the person speaking, make an effort to grasp their viewpoint, and then thoughtfully answer. Relationships are strengthened and good communication is promoted by active listening.

Develop a positive outlook on failure: Reframe your failure as a chance for personal development and education. Accept setbacks as stepping stones to achievement and use them into inspiration to keep going and get better.

Take part in self-care activities: Schedule time for mental, physical, and spiritual nourishment. This can involve things like going for walks in the outdoors, doing yoga or meditation, engaging in a favorite pastime, or treating oneself to a soothing bath.

Think about your values: Give your basic beliefs some thought and clarity. Your decisions, actions, and priorities will be guided by your understanding of what is genuinely important to you, which will result in a more authentic and fulfilling existence.

Honor and celebrate your accomplishments: Regardless of how big or small, take a minute to recognize and honor your accomplishments. Celebrating accomplishments gives you more self-assurance, strengthens constructive habits, and inspires you to keep improving.

Recall that personal development is an ongoing process. Select the concepts that speak to you and make them a part of your everyday existence. Make it a constant goal to better yourself, and approach the process of self-improvement with tolerance, tenacity, and self-compassion.

All of them are heartfelt remarks.

People genuinely fall in love with this gal.

"You're not supposed to frighten people!" Pretending not to be enraged, Mrs. Eva patted his hand without saying anything.

Kate turned back while she was speaking.

After taking a quick look at Andrew, Mrs. Eva turned around, picked up the watermelon she had just finished chopping, and moved in Kate's direction.

"You do realize how hot it is outside today? Eat some watermelon right now to stay cool."

Kate was given the watermelon by Mrs. Eva.

Kate, nevertheless, was only focused on Andrew standing behind her.

Now, whenever she sees Andrew, she is overcome with an innate anxiety and conflict and feels uneasy within, especially when she learns more rumors about him.

"Grandma, I."

Kate was about to finish when Mrs. Eva spoke out.

"What I said this morning doesn't count, just stay here, why do I have to move away!"

"Avoid moving at all." Mrs. Eva reiterated her affirmation.

After forcing Kate to return to the room, Mrs. Eva eventually approached her to offer her some fruit. She had a soft smile on her face the entire time, and her gait was exceptionally fluid.

Andrew's gaze paused momentarily, making it impossible to decipher his thoughts from his expression.

She heard Kate talking to someone when she walked past her room.

If you weren't paying close attention, you wouldn't be able to hear anything because the voice was so little and quiet.

"At first, I had trouble figuring out the issues in class. Three kids tried to sneak out this afternoon; I disciplined them, but they essentially ignored me."

I asked the principal as well, and he had no other option because "things in class are already chaotic, and I don't know what to do about the housing issue." I'm a terrible person who always gets people into trouble."

Kate gave a sadly audible sigh.

"What actions should I take?"

Kate asked that person, "Am I really bringing a lot of trouble to people?" because she was so miserable.

Kate thought it was appropriate when Andrew suggested she was disturbing the elderly. While Mrs. Eva cooks the rice, she peels the fruit for her. It's actually a little more problematic when there are multiple people living in the residence.

Additionally, there will be more activities...

She could not give Mrs. Eva any advice, even though she consistently insisted there was no need to.

Andrew merely paused outside the door before making his way back to his room.

I'm simply so irritated inside.

I want to beat someone, damn it.

It's gotten later than eleven.

Although Kate has completed her lesson plan, she does not intend to go to bed just yet.

She changed from her nightgown to long cotton clothing because it was getting cold at night.

Wearing this relaxed, comfy attire to bed is a great idea.

Hair was cleaned.

The wet hair reaches the neck and shoulders at the ends. The ends of your hair are also softly brushed when you droop your head.

After much internet research, she ultimately chose to concentrate on the system of rewards and penalties.

In fact, discipline is now more crucial than instruction. No matter how effectively you educate, it will be for naught if the discipline is poor.

She discovered a ton of notes online and studied other people's approaches.

I simply took notes in a notepad this entire evening, but nearly half of them were written down.

It would take some time to rearrange everything, she thought.

I'm not sure when I'll be able to sleep tonight.

She switched only the little light on while sitting at the table, leaving the large light off.

The only sound in the calm room was the sound of the pen being pressed against the paper. The space was lit by soft golden light.

Kate writes with a lot of emotion.

The sound of footsteps suddenly became audible at this point. When she heard it, she was astounded and stopped moving her hands as well.

Her ears perked up, and she paid close attention.

A rustling, impacting sound.

Kate somewhat imagined that her heart stopped, so she bravely put down the pen and looked in the direction of the sound.

That noise is beneath the table.

A "chirp" noise.

Whiteness shot across Kate's face.

A dark shadow moved from her feet, tail up, and slid under the bed as she bowed her head.

She truly noticed it this time.

Kate tried not to panic as she heard the noise beneath the bed growing louder and louder, nearly retreating as fast as she could to the door.

Where the bed is the furthest away.

Mice are Kate's worst phobia.

She had been afraid since infancy and eventually turned into a ghost. Her hands and feet were cold, and she would shake with horror every time she spotted a mouse.

She would have called out for help if this had been her home.

However, because this was someone else's home, she took care to avoid upsetting anyone else and didn't even dare to speak.

Kate was terrified, yet she continued to stare toward the bed.

She consumed bread with a few crumbs during the day. A black animal jumped and continued to make "squeaking" noises in a dimly lit nook.

This sound was almost going to knock Kate out.

She drew breath and began to cry as a tear the size of a bean dropped with a "drop" sound.

She also felt so worthless that it was becoming too much for her.

At this precise moment, a dark silhouette "suddenly" moved in her direction.

"Aha!" Kate let out a scream uncontrollably.

My back had already touched the door when I turned around.

"What commotion!" Angry but still managing to keep his voice down,

Andrew kicked the door outside and aggressively exclaimed, "It's night, don't you know that the old man is already asleep?"

It truly defies comprehension.

"Shut up!" Once more, Trinh Phong bellowed loudly.

He exuded a murderous atmosphere due to his black T-shirt, serious short hair, dark breath, and angry aura coupled with the color of the night.

The man was really vicious, but in that instant Kate felt like a drowning person who reached for a stake, turned to face him, and yelled, "There are rats in the room."

Andrew has always had extremely sensitive ears.

A sequence of odd, disorganized noises filled the room, and he also heard some sobbing mixed in with voices. Startled, he opened the door.

After walking outside, Kate looked up in a fright when she noticed the tall person in front of her, and their eyes briefly locked.

She hurried to get behind him without giving it any thought.

As if there were no reason to be terrified if you were hiding behind someone else's back.

With one hand gripping the corner of his shirt, Kate recoiled in retreat.

Then I let go right away after remembering something.

Andrew swiveled his head to look.

All I could see of her was her entire body tucked beneath him, securely concealed, still, and unmoving.

After taking several long breaths and attempting to quiet her mind, Kate opened her mouth to ask, "Can you... help me chase it away?"

She had to set her fear and depression aside now that she is in this predicament and has gone through something similar.

Solving the current issue is of utmost importance.

Certainly, she was unable to eradicate the mice on her own.

It's only Andrew who can assist her here.

With her chin lowered and her snow-white skin standing out in the darkness, Kate's little and attractive form, dressed in a loose nightgown, exuded vitality and alertness.

She has flawless, porcelain-white complexion that is incredibly gorgeous and flawless.

With its concealing appearance, fluttering eyelashes, and drooping eyes, it particularly looks like a kitten.

A beggarly kitten on the run is pleading for help.

Yes, pleading for covert action.

can quickly pique people's need for security.

Going to work on Monday morning in my favorite skinny jeans and a fresh white top felt luxury after spending the whole weekend drenched in perspiration, dust, and the spiderwebs I kept finding. I looked like an entirely different person with my hair down in all of its crazy red beauty and full makeup. I also had that same scent.

However, I felt strangely unsatisfied as I put my coffee and handbag down at my cubicle in the Booms & Nibbles offices' corner where the marketing staff worked. Why was it that a part of me wanted to be collaborating with Troy on the house project? Usually, I would have been more than content to let him finish it as I left for my day job. However, I had considered going over to get him some coffee today, but given the state of the house, there was no way I could leave without getting soiled in some way.

My buddy Angela stopped by and took a seat on the edge of my desk before I had a chance to investigate the impulse too much. "You will never believe who Tessa chose to replace her as the head of marketing."

I gave her a smile and settled into my chair, eager to listen to the newest drama in the workplace.

Almost every day has delivered something exciting since the business owner hired a consultant a few months ago. Initially, it was the consultant—the kind of man that dreams are made of. I had made an attempt to get close to him, but he was now seeing Tessa, our new C.E.O. When it originally surfaced, it had been shocking—especially when we learned that Krista, her assistant, was seeing Tessa's ex-boyfriend—but it was all old news at this point.

"All right, who is it?"

"A male."

My jaw fell agape. "What?"

"I promise. Additionally, he's Whistling, she pressed her lips together. "We don't yet know if he is single." Although I haven't gotten an opportunity to speak with him, I saw him at Tessa's office.

You know that she hired him, but how?

"I was told by Krista."

Normally, Krista was not so much an information source as she was a steel-faced bar bouncer. "She could not have given up the information."

Yes, she did. I got to meet him when he left Tessa's office after that. But there was no way I was going to give her the real story. Additionally, you'll soon get to meet him. Have you noticed that we are meeting in a short while?

Not at all. My email hasn't been checked yet this morning.

Yes, we do. Now I'm going there to secure an excellent seat. I'll make an effort to get his attention.

"All right, then no calling dibs."

We both know there won't be a second date, so I'll just wait to go for him after your first one.

Even though I knew she was kidding, her remark hit home because she was correct. "Yes, well, I've just been unlucky lately."

"Your misfortune presents me with a chance. I hope to see you inside.

I muttered, "See ya," as she turned to leave.

I realized that Angela was correct when I looked at my phone's email. With a humming sense of interest, I grabbed my tablet and made my way down the corridor, knowing I just had a few minutes to make it to the conference room. Tessa could not have recruited anybody deserving of I'm starting to get competitive with Angela. When a single attractive man showed up at our all-female office the last time, it completely rocked the place. There's no way we could get this fortunate again. Which man desired to be employed by a lingerie company?

Nevertheless, I accelerated my pace since I was eager to learn. I rounded the curve at top speed and collided head-on with a person approaching from the opposite way. My ankle turned sideways in the impact, I dropped my phone and tablet, powerful hands gripped my arms, and icy liquid splattered all over me.

I gasped as I peered down at the black, frothy material pressing against my flesh and seeping into my thin white blouse. Coke.

"Whoa, that guy over there." "Are you alright?"

I knew it was a man even with all else I'd had to digest. His hands wrapped around my entire upper arm in a steadying yet somehow soft hold that no woman could pull off. The chest I had smacked felt substantial.

Now let's get to know the new marketing chief.

I saw a face etched with beautiful angles when I looked up. Sharp and slender, but softened by large eyes and lips that were currently abnormally open. His thick black hair spilled forward over his forehead, and a pair of big, thin-framed glasses sat precariously on the edge of his nose.

Yes, I said, my lengthy pause being far too noticeable. I apologize. I turned that corner far too quickly.

"I was also in a rush." Then he gave me a sidelong glance, released me, and abruptly withdrew his hands. He knelt and scooped up my phone and tablet, holding them up to me with one hand while he grabbed up the open Coke bottle that was now dripping into the floor, leaving a foamy mess.

A few feet away, I watched as he located the Coke lid and twisted it back on before looking helplessly at the carpet. My clothing was the greater concern for me. I looked down at my chest and tentatively peeled the transparent, brown cloth away from my skin. It landed soggily against my skin once again when I released it. When it dried, I was going to be a sticky mess.

I checked out my electronics after noticing they were far more pricey than my blouse. A few drips were scattered among them, primarily on the tablet's cover. They would be alright.

I looked up again, and there he was, standing in front of me, his lips tight and his jaw tightened. I took advantage of the opportunity to examine his naked ring finger as he clutched the mostly empty coke bottle in his left hand. He followed my gaze in that direction. He made an embarrassing joke, saying, "Well, at least it wasn't coffee."

It was easy to grin at him, even if it made me uneasy. "That was undoubtedly going to have been worse."

With a wave of his hand toward my breast, he eventually replied, "I want to fix this, but I'm not sure how."

"Never fear. By coincidence, my automobile has a change of clothes in it.

Although it's not really business casual, this will be preferable to it.

He became somewhat at ease. At least you are lucky. What can I do to make up for this, though, still?

Undoubtedly, I ought to have dismissed his worries and reassured him that everything was alright, but in the unlikely event that he was unmarried, I could not let this opportunity slip away. He had an aristocratic yet geeky look, and it wasn't just the spectacles. His intelligent eyes shone brightly. Still, he reminded me of an actor from a Korean drama—tall and incredibly beautiful—even though I had no idea what Asian nation his family was from.

"How about we discuss that at a later time? You weren't exactly in a rush, did you?

He gave a blink. "I was." Are you certain? I probably shouldn't have arrived late for my first meeting because I forgot something in my office. He gave a brief pause before continuing, "Today is my first day."

I chuckled. "I don't need you to tell me that. It's quite clear because there aren't any other men in the office."

"All right."

I moved backward to give him space and gestured to send him away when he persisted in his hesitation. "Go ahead. I'm alright. Please just stand up for me if Tessa questions me about why I'm late.

With a long finger, he gestured at me and turned to leave. "Unquestionably."

I bit my lip to contain the amused smile that was attempting to take across my face as I followed him. It appeared as though fate had worked in my favor.

6 Bryce

We have until 7:30 to meet the other couples. I don't understand Denise's want to arrive so early. I agree to meet her at the desk an hour early because it seems like a pointless argument.

Isabella gives me a smile as she sees me coming. "Denise instructed me to inform you that she will be leaving in a short while." She points to some upholstered chairs on the other side.

I select the chair that faces the desk directly. Denise comes flying around the rear corner with a pile of paperwork. She takes a seat next to Isabella and works.

Isabella gives me a sorry-looking smile and softened eyes, as if she knows Denise won't be here for a little while.

It's not what we're doing. I approach Denise and take a position just in front of her. She doesn't even raise her gaze.

I tap the desk twice. "What are you doing?"

Her focus remains on the pages in front of her as she responds, "Let me just finish this and then we can go."

When you were ready to go, why didn't you just ask me to come down?

"I dislike arriving late."

I bend over the desk to have a closer look at her outfit.

"You will cause yourself to be late. Are you not in need of changing? I inquire.

What do you mean? I'm clothed. At last, her attention drifts from her work and she stares down at her clothes. Her eyebrows furrow in a questioning manner. It is only James and those two. I have no desire to win over anyone.

Fuck me, then, huh?

She's dressed in a polished, pinstriped business casual. Although I have nothing against folks dressing however they feel most comfortable, she isn't going to have me out here looking insane. Who shows up at a bowling alley wearing a business suit? That stuff won't be happening to my arm.

I move to face Isabella. "Isabella, how long have you worked here?"

Isabella must have been surprised by my question. She turns to face Denise, who nods and shrugs, saying it's alright to respond. "Six years."

"A three-year period is quite long." My elbow rests on the desk. "How much of a friend would you say you are?"

Isabella warily glances over at Denise, who is still scribbling away at her paperwork, and says, "I mean, she's my boss."

"How recently has she gone on a date?"

Denise's daze is broken by that. "There is no date here."

I correct her and turn back to Isabella, saying, "I didn't say this was a date and I asked Isabella not you." "When did you last witness her going on a date?"

She stares up at the ceiling as if she's looking through her memory vault, putting two fingertips to her lips. "Never."

"It's not a date," Denise says once more.

I ignore Denise and carry on talking to Isabella. "What sort of evening do you suppose she'll have in that?"

Denise smacks her pen across the surface.

I reassure Isabella, "Don't worry about her," and wave the back of my palm in Denise's direction. "Please tell me where you think she's going to be tonight."

"A dinner for business?"

My eyes glaze over. That's right. In any case, what is she working on?

"The schedule," responds Isabella.

"For the following week?"

"The next year," she murmurs.

"Oh my god, no." I return my slide and grab those papers from Denise. Give this garbage to me. Come on, let's go.

"What are you doing?" Her voice rings through the deserted lobby.

"From here, how far is it to the bowling alley?" I ask Isabella the question.

"About five minutes,"

I use my phone to check the time. Alright. Come on, let's go.

"We've got time." Denise reaches for the files once more.

"You're accurate. We can get you something to wear in the time we have left. I look back over at Isabella. "Will you please finish this?"

"The schedule is the same every time." Isabella chuckles as she removes my hands from the schedule.

As if Isabella has betrayed her, Denise narrows her gaze at her. "You ought to be on my side," I said.

"Yes, I am. Go have fun. Isabella ejects Denise.

I'm grateful, Isabella.

I extend a hand to Denise. Playfully, she smacks it away. With a big handbag in one hand and a grey bowling bag in the other, she ducks under the desk and stands back up. She round the desk so that I can see everything she believes to be proper bowling apparel.

She can't mean business.

It's not a romantic outing. Denise responds, "I don't know why you're so concerned about my clothes," as soon as we get outside.

It's true that this isn't a date. I recall your guidelines. I tell her, "But we're still one of three couples, and I want us to be the most attractive."

Searching her purse for her keys, she tries to pull away from me.

"Where are you heading? I tell her, "We're right here," gesturing to the valet who is holding open the door to my rental.

"I am capable of driving. All you have to do is follow me. I am aware of the path," she says.

The GPS concurs. And I said, 'We have to find you something to wear first.'"

She pauses, takes a moment to examine herself, then glances at her watch. "I have no time to change all the way home."

"Somewhere within a reasonable distance, there's probably a mall."

Actually, it makes no difference what she wears. Either way, she looks great. The issue is that, when we go out to bowl a few frames and have a few drinks, it appears as though she will bargain for a raise.

"I'm not going to buy a new wardrobe just to go bowling. It isn't really profound.

"You're accurate. It's not that profound," I concur. "I'm going to get you something cozier to wear."

I'm rejected by Denise. "I don't require anything from you."

"I didn't pose a question. Denise, get in the car.

"Bryce, it's not that bad. They are aware of my wardrobe.

I take a deep breath and move in close enough that her chin almost touches my chest while she cranes to look up at me. She puts her weight on one leg and crosses her arms over her chest. Even though I'm right up on her, she doesn't move.

"Denise, get in the car. I replied, "I understand."

Her face contorted in defiant opposition, she stands.

"Denise."

"Bryce."

We wait to see who will cave in first while we stand there in silent defiance. I'm not breaking, so we're just going to be two idiots standing outside this motel.

It's the valet who speaks. "Well. Sir?

I tell her, "I'm not doing this with you."

I bend over her and pick her up, carrying her over my shoulder before she can make her next comeback. In one form or another, she is getting into this car.

With a gasp, Denise rattles out a few things that don't really interest me. Please put me down, Bryce. You know I can drive myself, right? You're truly insane.

Her tiny heels give me a kick. I carefully set her in the car, using my free arm to still them.

The valet is unsure about how to proceed. He shuts his boss's door after apologizing to her. I walk around to the driver's side and give him a twenty. I stifle a grin and celebrate the tiny triumph. She is not a woman who is easily defeated.

When the car syncs to my phone's playlist, she looks at the radio while Earth, Wind, and Fire plays over the speakers.

"Really?" With a frown, Denise queries.

How come? You find it objectionable? I inquire.

She says, "I just wasn't expecting it."

How come? Did you expect me to be listening to trap music? I clench my jaw. "Before you go making assumptions, you should probably take a few minutes to get to know me." I give her a finger shake and direct the GPS to a mall that's close by.

She scans the cabin of the vehicle. How is the car doing?

It was my music at first, and now it's my car. What issues does my car have? I inquire.

"Who is the Range Rover renter? You have just a few days in this city. You were unable to choose something simple?

"Oh." I let out a brief puff of breath in laughter. "This is my vehicle. Not this one, naturally. However, I already have one at home. The simple things provide a sense of normalcy when you're traveling as frequently as I do. At the light, I turn left. "No matter where I travel, I always rent the same car."

"That makes sense." She gives a shrug.

I'm excited about tonight. I haven't spent much time with folks I don't work with in a long time. And the further I travel, the fewer and farther between those times are. As the years go by, it seems more and more like the life I vowed I'd never have—one where I'm constantly traveling and never really at home.

"What prompted you to accept my invitation?" When the first song ends, I inquire.

The smile on BRAYDEN R.ein Petty's face froze me in my tracks. I didn't even realize Rein was one of the two young women Emmett was sitting with until I went over to greet him. Now she was a woman. Her lips were still large and rosy, and her cheeks were still lovely and plump when she smiled, but in some way, everything else about her had changed.

The way she made my tongue feel thick in my mouth was amazing.

Even though she was seated and her lower body was concealed by the table, her contours were still visible. Her hair, formerly dark and raven-black, was now splattered with vivid red columns. Her eyes shone brightly, and her lashes were lengthy.

"Dude, come sit down." Pulling out the chair, Emmett moved it away from Rein. "There will be more food on its way.

Would you like me to summon the waitress so you may place your order as well?

"I think I'll just grab a drink," I said, hoping that the one empty chair wasn't the one next to Rein. I think she thought the same thing.

If so, she didn't express it. I settled into the chair next to her as she grabbed for her beer and savored it.

Gracie looked at me and remarked, "So, Hennie Enterprises," resting her chin on her knuckles. "How is that going?"

Emmett gave her a menacing glance. "The dude arrived just now. Can't you have the grace to speak with him about something other than work straight away?

Gracie furrowed her brow. "Very nice tee. How did you obtain it?

What? I enquired. "I can't recall—"

That's alright, Gracie said. Hennie Enterprises, then. How is that proceeding? A sly smirk curved the corner of her mouth.

I laughed and combed through my hair with my fingers. Gracie is the one who gets right to the point. That's what I had always appreciated about her. She was a girl who didn't put up with crap. She was extremely excellent for Rein when they were younger ladies in high school, I remembered. She enabled her to express herself.

"It's good," I murmured. "It brings in money."

"Seemingly," Gracie pondered, glancing at me. "You have to be kind."

Like everything, it has advantages and disadvantages. The impulse to tell her that she was exactly as bitchy as I recalled was strong in me. "My time is mostly occupied with work. To be quite honest, this is the first time in more than four years that I have sat down at a bar for a drink that wasn't related to a work meeting. I'm not able to stay for too long, even now. I must return to my daughter.

"She's adorable," Emmett remarked, gently prodding my elbow with his. "What is her age?"

"Four."

Grace added, "Emmett was telling us a bit about her earlier." "Bella is her name?"

I gave a nod.

"Where is her mother? Are you back in Florida? She must be relishing the opportunity to have the place all to herself. With a laugh, Gracie grabbed her beer and took a taste of the foamy top.

I moved in my chair. "Bella's mother passed away during childbirth," I said, sensing the abrupt shift in the atmosphere. This was something I detested. I detested all of it: the sympathy, the pity, and the excuses. "Bela and I are fine; it was a long time ago."

"I ought not to have—" Gracie got going.

I extended my hand. It's alright. You were unaware.

I ordered a whiskey on the rocks, and the waitress showed there just in time. Soon after, she brought it back, and I ignored how awkward everyone was now at the table as I took a sip. I couldn't hold it against Rein because she hadn't said a word to me yet. Had I not felt like such a jerk sitting next to her, I would have had the guts to say something first.

Nervousness made me drink the whiskey faster than I meant to.

I turned to Emmett and felt Rein's eyes on me after dropping the empty glass onto the table a bit too forcefully. I apologize, but I must go back. It was pleasant to see you all again.

Gracie sat staring up at me, both eyebrows shooting up toward her hairline. "You're heading off so quickly? We hardly had time to converse. You didn't even inquire as to our activities. She made a lovely pout out of her red lips.

"Apologies, fatherhood demands."

Gracie leaned back in her chair, shrugging her shoulders. Nobody is able to dispute that. You've probably used it to escape a number of awkward circumstances.

A hint of awkwardness appeared, and I saw Rein's head snap toward Gracie. I put my hands into my jeans pockets and swayed back on my heels as the two women exchanged a gaze that took me back to my childhood. "I've used it once or twice in a pinch."

With a tense laugh, Emmett smacked his knee. "It's up to you to make an excuse for your daughter."

"Not at this moment."

Emmett stood up and gave me a hearty pat on the back. Well, whatever the case, it was good to see you. Do you anticipate remaining in this world for a little while longer?

Indeed. A little.

Good to know, Emmett replied. Call me at any moment, or come over to the diner. I will prepare the tastiest cheeseburger your daughter has ever tasted.

I chuckled. "Good luck convincing her to consume meat."

Emmett let out a gasp. Not at all. Were any of those crazy vegetarian kids raised by you?

Bella won't eat anything that formerly had a face, but I doubt she even understands what a vegetarian is.

"How cute is that?" Gracie sighed.

"It's annoying," I said. "It pains me to make sure she eats enough."

Gracie remarked, "I believe every daughter is a pain in her father's ass."

I said, "I won't argue with you on that one."

I cast a quick glance at Rein, who continued to stare away from me. I attempted to look her in the eye, but she stayed still, staring at Gracie. I chided myself; say anything to her, you idiot. However, the words never seemed to come. Years had passed since I first left Valdez, and I had been thinking about her and all the things I should have said to her, beginning with "I'm sorry." But I couldn't imagine how pitiful an apology would sound coming out of my mouth now that she was standing right in front of me, looking more gorgeous than ever, and not even bothering to look at me. It was ten fucking years ago. She had good cause to despise me.

"I will see you guys soon," I murmured, turning away from the table.

Gracie and Emmett both said, "Bye."

I detested having to strain my ears to listen for Rein's voice over theirs. I was unable to.

I headed right for the front doors, reaching up to take my jacket off the hanger. I slid my arms into the jacket after putting on my gloves. I took one more glance back at the table as I finished buttoning the collar.

Rein and I met eyes.

With my fingers tucked under my chin, I froze as the final button went through the opening. Rein's eyebrows furrowed as her eyes grew wide and she cast a critical glance down at the table.

I turned to face her and gently opened the door, going outside into the chilly evening air.

I was reminded of the reason I had left this little small town behind with every step I took through the snow on the pavement.

The lack of activities in Valdez provided little relief from the weather, and the cold was an annoyance that never went away. I had been craving something more for the entire time I had been here. I've always known that small-town existence couldn't be all there is. There was no challenge that Valdez could provide for me.

Ten years had a weird way of changing your memory of the past, and Rein had been collateral damage. It brought back memories of how deeply I had cared for her before, and how wonderful our time together had been, to see her now.

When the chance to flee Dodge presented itself, I suppose it hadn't been good enough for me to cling to.

"Please take this soda."

I glance down at the Pepsi can and up at Darla. "I'll get by."

"Oh, it's just sugar, give me a break." My fingers are wrapped around the cold can as Darla takes hold of my hand. "Garcia is very concerned because you haven't eaten anything since the morning."

"Well, at least she seems to care about me."

"Explain yourself," exclaims Darla. "I also care about you."

I grind my teeth to be succinct. It's challenging to determine. For instance, instead of giving me ice drink in this freezing weather, you ought to be cuddling me with a steaming mug of something warm.

"How ungrateful," Darla mocks. "You ought to be grateful that I'm in your life. You are unworthy of me.

"I concur. I'm worthy of much more.

"Whoa, what a bitch."

With a loud laugh stifled, I lay back down. Even though the sand is still wet from yesterday's downpour and the beach is empty, I enjoy the feeling of the cold against my skin. Rocky Cove hasn't had a day without rain in almost a month. Today is ideal for moping and wallowing in the pain caused by Joe's treachery.

Joe is selling the guesthouse and is moving on. What an asshole.

"Skiee, I'm not sure. Although we understand how devoted you are to the location, you cannot stay there indefinitely.

"Darla, that's not the point."

"Moreover," she brusquely cuts me off. Joe is the owner, no matter what. Whether or not to sell it is entirely up to him. It's a good thing he made a compromise with Devon Gray to have you around.

"I'm not sure how acquisition operates like that. Furthermore, I am not a thing that can be transferred from one business owner to another.

Then give up! It's not a problem at all, Skye. Joe needed to pay his expenses. He was even lent money!

I scoff at the prompt. "The fact that he didn't update me on our money until yesterday is not my responsibility. Joe tried to pay off a large loan for years, but he kept it a secret from me! He informed me that it was a lottery.

Darla gives a nod. Yeah, telling that fib was a mistake. He ought to have just told the truth.

And finally, a consensus. Joe has been responsible for repaying a loan on his own for the past ten years, having lied to a thirteen-year-old. You believe that you know a man. "He can go to Asia and whaling for the rest of his life, that's all I care about," you say. I'm going to live my life.

Darla pulls me close, putting her palm across my chest. He must be really regretful for what he did to you. On the other hand, there is a request for your visit from someone at the front desk. Payton, West."

I jerk upright and snap her hand off. "What?"

Indeed, Darla replies, "He's been waiting for a while now."

"Are you insane? You have a guest, and you remained silent the entire time? I get up quickly and brush the damp sand off my thighs.

I've never seen you show such urgency for a guy. Does this mean I should know anything? Darla stands up and asks a question.

I give her the drink can in response, then I leave.

"SKYE!" she yells back at me. "I was only kidding! NO ONE IS IN THE RECEPTION AREA!

Emma and Luke's confidence in each other grew as their friendship did. Their shared experiences and ability to trust one another to reveal their vulnerabilities and pasts became the foundation of their relationship.

Emma decided it was time to concentrate on her own insecurities and dreams one quiet night as they sat on the yard of her childhood house, the sea waves providing a comforting backdrop. She talked of her childhood desires, the dreams of being a craftswoman that she had to put off, and the fear of continuing to live an unfulfilled life on a daily basis.

Emma admitted, revealing a vulnerability she had never shared with anyone, "I've usually felt like I'm drifting through life, that I'm missing something. I thought that being with Imprint would provide me with stability, but instead of pursuing what truly fulfills me, I can't help but feel tempted to wonder if I have consented to something protected."

Luke listened intently, the words echoing back to him from his own struggles. He too had aspirations that he had abandoned, and a series of unexpected setbacks had marked his life. He spoke softly and honestly about his own experiences, the frustrations he overcame, and his fear of repeating mistakes from the past.

Their revelations brought them closer together, twirling around a tapestry of common experiences and comprehension. They talked about the weight of societal presumptions, their fears of taking on new challenges, and their desire for something different in their lives.

Their conversations dragged on for the ensuing lengthy periods. Emma pushed Luke to come back to his creative spirit, and he gave her his portraits and artwork, revealing a talent that had long been hidden. Luke, therefore, inspired Emma to pick up her paintbrush once more, kindling the creative spark she had all but forgotten.

Their late-night conversations under the stars became a haven for their souls, a place where they could let go of their uncertainties and anxieties. They discovered they could be who they truly were without fear of being judged, and they took solace in one other's company.

But every moment of vulnerability they shared made their desire for one another stronger. Never again could they ignore the electric charge that seemed to surround them whenever they got near. Unquestionably, their friendship had grown into something more complex, a powerful blend of understanding, friendship, and a certain amount of sincere pressure.

In the midst of their confessions and the growing attraction between them, Emma and Luke were teetering on the precipice. The decisions they made next would determine how their lives would unfold and how deeply they would love one other.

Remember to provide an unbiased evaluation.

Chapter 6: The Moonlit Dancing Night

"The Night of the Moonlit Dance," the sixth chapter of "The Journey of the First Kiss," is a fantastic continuation of Jane and David's developing romance. This chapter is a stunning fusion of suspense, revelry, and the enduring allure of a high school dance held outside beneath the stars.

The announcement of the yearly high school Moonlight Dance opens the chapter. Excitement permeates the entire institution. Jane and David are excited to go to the dance together as they continue to explore their new relationship.

Jane and David experience mixed emotions as they go closer to the dancing. Both of them want the evening to be exceptional and unforgettable. With the assistance of her pals, Jane spends hours choosing the ideal clothing, and David picks up some dancing skills.

The story does a fantastic job of capturing the range of feelings that Jane and David go through leading up to dance night. Every little detail, from choosing the ideal attire to perfecting the dancing routines, increases their anticipation.

The Moonlight Dancing Day finally arrives. Soft music is playing as the high school hall is exquisitely decked with sparkling lights. Jane appears ethereal in her silver dress under the moonlight. With his timeless black suit on, David can't take his eyes off Jane. His heart leaps at the sight of Jane, which only serves to confirm how much he loves her.

The dance is the chapter's high point. David and Jane experience a stunning, life-changing event as they hit the dance floor. Under the moonlight, they sway to the beat of the music, their hearts beating in unison. They have a strong connection, and they dance together for the first time as a couple, signifying their newly discovered love.

Following their enthralling dance, they withdraw to the terrace to avoid the commotion of the celebration. As the moon and stars twinkle, they sit in cozy silence, holding hands and lost in their own world. Their emotional intimacy is heightened by this moment of pure connection and silent understanding that they have together in the stillness of the night.

There is a lot of emotional depth in the dialogue that Jane and David are having outside. They deepen their relationship by talking about their concerns, dreams, and common history. They discuss their future together, not with any set plans, but with the understanding that they see each other in it. This exchange reflects how their relationship has developed over time and shows how they have matured as a couple.

Jane starts to cry a little because she is so moved by David and the beauty of the night. David wipes away her tears in an emotional moment, his gaze full of affection and his touch soft. Despite its simplicity, this private moment is very important to them as they prepare for their first kiss.

The chapter also discusses how their friends and peers feel about their developing romance. Noticing a change in their connection, they encounter taunts and lighthearted remarks. But in between the jokes and laughs, their friends also say how happy and supportive they are of Jane and David.

As Chapter 6 comes to an end, David and Jane are filled with optimism and eagerness for their future together, vowing to create more priceless moments together. A wonderful scene concludes with David kissing Jane gently on the forehead in the glow of the stars. This gives the night of the moonlit dance a lovely conclusion by making Jane and David blush and feel their hearts race.

"The Night of the Moonlit Dance" highlights the emotional connection and reciprocal love between Jane and David and provides a closer look into their romantic journey. The viewer is left excitedly expecting their much-awaited first kiss after reading this chapter, which is rather engaging.

Why do I keep having these experiences? Am I a horrible person? No, am I the world's worst person?

"Avoid being ridiculous." Myles grabs my phone out of my grasp. "And give up gazing at it. You're only making yourself more anxious.

I grab my Strawberry Oreo milkshake and take a sip, moaning.

We're at our favorite weekend haunt, a charming corner café on Main Street in Alcott Bay. Fortunately, none of our other students have arrived yet. Our junior class is not the only one that comes here often.

However, I'm not here to hang out with the gals alone. I woke up to like a million notifications this morning. The origin?a picture on Instagram in which I was mentioned. Stupid Kayla shared a picture of Dean and me in his room on social media, writing, "Oops! I apologize for upsetting you two.

The shouting at the top of my lungs was something I could hardly control.

The only bright spot is that Riley won't ever see it and can't show our parents what Kayla did because she didn't post it on TikTok. All I can say is that I'm relieved Dad has completely forgotten about our scheduled conversation. In that regard, I'm completely OK as long as my sister doesn't remind him.

"Fin, don't worry. With a tongue-click, Serena assures me, "We already reported it. It still amazes me that Kayla shared the photo. What was going through her mind?

Ever since Luke Benson asked her out last year, she has had it out for Finley. Remember how Kayla has been crushing on him since the sixth grade?

"Oh, I see. Serena gives a nod. "Had she not cried in the girls' restroom?"

"Really?" I snicker. "She sobbed because of the guy who frequently burps the alphabet? Can't she find a better person to develop feelings for?

Myles chuckles. "They say what you know. The heart desires what it desires.

I frown. Well, I'm not interested in what her heart desires. That boy doesn't appeal to me at all.

Kayla is aware of this. That's probably why she despises you. Because you're not into the boy she wants, even though he likes you.

Before taking a drink of her Rocky Road milkshake, Serena gives another click of her tongue. "Bad girl."

"What do you know? Let's stop discussing her now. After all, she is the reason we are here. What action will I take? Everyone believes that Dean and I hooked up.

"Anyway, what were you doing in his room?" Myles queries.

"What made him wear no shirt?" Serena interjects. "We apologize, but you still haven't responded to these questions."

Yes, I didn't give them a detailed explanation of anything. I simply informed them that Jace and Kayla had observed us in that manner. I went upstairs to avoid him after spotting him in the crowd. I did, however, wind up in his room. I had no idea he would find me there. Regarding the portion without a shirt, I'm clueless. Was he going to put on a new shirt, perhaps? Plus, he might have forgotten because I was present. Really, does it matter?

Serena responds, "Well, everyone who saw Kayla's post does."

Myles advises me, "You ought to speak with Dean." "He can assist you in resolving this matter. Well, he ought should. He is also a part of it. Additionally, if you cooperate to persuade everyone of the truth, perhaps it will seem more plausible.

"Or I can just wait for the problem to go away."

In any case, I owe no one an explanation. The important thing is that I be aware of the truth. Correct?

I kept spinning in my head. Nick simply drove us to an Italian restaurant without asking where I wanted to go. Renowned Italian eatery Cinzzetti's is renowned for its genuine cuisine. I had heard it was both extremely costly and amazing.

So I bit my lower lip in nervousness when he parked. There were a lot of reasons why I didn't want to be here right now, even if I had never been to Cinzzetti's before. I dressed way too casually for a posh restaurant like this one. Not including tips, it also cost more than I make in five hours. In addition, I was anxious just because I was with Nick in such a fine setting. This is not the spot to get lunch after work, but rather to take someone on a date!

Nick scowled at me and said, "What's the matter?" as he opened my door.

I pivoted to gaze upward at the hand he extended. I accepted it, and he got me out of the car with ease. Standing next to him, I turned to face myself. I muttered, "I'm not dressed for this place."

He laughed and answered, "It's not some formal dining place." It's buffet style, so while some guests will be dressed formally, others will be more casually attired. You're alright.

The last sentence sounded more like something he was saying to me than it did about my clothes. That was really nice! "All right, if you're sure."

He guided me toward the door by placing his hand on the small of my back. "I'm positive. To boot, I wanted to show you what authentic Italian cuisine tastes like. There is nothing better than Cinzzetti's.

I was relieved to see that there were, in fact, individuals dressed casually when we first arrived. The feast was an understatement given the stunning surroundings. It resembled tiny Italian city blocks with a variety of cuisines located on each block. I had the impression that I was strolling around the streets of Italy because of the vibrant flags and decorations.

Before I could get my wallet out of my mouth, Nick led the way to the hostess, where he made his payment. The hostess motioned for us to follow her, and Nick's hand instantly returned to my back.

A waiter met us right away at the table. Would we like to try the house wine, he asked? With a laugh, Nick remarked, "She's not twenty-one." Nick ordered sodas, and the server returned in a short while, grinning.

He turned to go toward an Italian street and said, "Come on." He gestured at a sign. Every station has a sign indicating its offerings. You can order anything you want from the chefs. Never have I come here and not been able to get what I asked for." After guiding me around the bend, he pointed out two side streets, the salad street, three main course streets, and not just one, but two dessert streets.

I exclaimed, taking everything in. "I'm not sure if I'm truly hungry enough to consume everything I want to."

Chuckling, Nick pointed me back in the direction of the main dish streets. "Well, we'll return if you don't get to try everything you want to."

I forcefully gulped. He would bring me back? It felt too good to be true, after months and months of hoping things like this would materialize. I most definitely didn't want to ruin it by making a dumb comment about his girlfriend. Nope. Anybody I could take, I would.

Picking up a plate each, we filled them straight from the main course streets. I obtained samples of several items in an attempt to try as many as possible. Upon sitting down, we both seemed to be more interested in the meal than in talking, which alarmed me.

Nick glanced up and gave me a wink after clearing his plate. "Do you enjoy it?"

I nodded and said, "Yes." I frowned and continued, "But I knew this was going to happen."

Nick's lips curved downward and his gaze squinted. "What could possibly go wrong?"

I laughed aloud. "As soon as I saw all the food, I knew I wouldn't be eating any sides or salad. There would only be main courses and desserts. As though to hide, I bowed my head and turned in my shoulders. I muttered, "Is that okay?" as I sucked in the corner of my lower lip.

The laughter relaxed me and filled the air. With ease, Nick helped me get out of the chair by standing up and taking hold of my hand. He responded, "Of course it's okay," as he reached up and delicately touched my lip with the pad of his thumb before releasing it from my grasp. "Have I ever told you that when you do that, I want to suck your lip into my own mouth?" he added, leaning in close.

I felt a chill run up my spine and I stopped cold. Nick laughed once again and drew me into a small alcove that was off limits to most people. Just before he bent over and accomplished exactly what he had indicated he intended, he took his thumb and ran it lightly across my lower lip. My lower lip got caught in his entire mouth. Before he sealed his lips around it and swallowed my full lip, his teeth teased along it. He touched my lip again with his tongue, and my entire body tingled.

My body trembled, my legs went squishy, and my heart raced. His body laughed in response.

How on earth was he able to laugh? When I opened my eyes, he was smiling and said, "Are you okay? You shuddered. Do you feel chilly?

He was well aware that I wasn't frigid. All I could say was "Um."

Nick leaned up close once more. He muttered, "I also like it when I leave you speechless," and led the way to the streets of dessert, where I filled my plate to the brim with practically everything.

I slumped back in my chair and moaned when we had eaten as much as we could. I'm so full, it's ridiculous. Why did you allow me to have another crepe with strawberries and cream?

Nick laughed. He raised an eyebrow and continued, "I don't think you realize how fun it was to watch you eat them."

I lacked the energy to appreciate his compliment or feel ashamed. Rather, I said, "I need a nap," as I closed my eyes.

Nick put his hand in mine and led the way to his car, saying, "That can be arranged." He pressed a lever to get inside, and the seat almost fell back. He shut the door behind him and climbed in, reclining his seat to match mine.

He said, "This way," taking a jacket out of the back seat. He placed it beneath my head after folding it.

I rolled on my side and faced him, saying, "Thank you." And I'm grateful for the dinner. I'm able to reimburse you.

Nick chuckled. "I want no payment from you. You're welcome as well.

We exchanged long looks for quite some time. which, strangely enough, wasn't an unpleasant situation for me. I think it's a mix of being exhausted and really enjoying his company.

Is the temperature too high? He raised an arm to rest his head and inquired, "I can turn on the air conditioning."

It was difficult to realize that so many months had gone by since my initial encounter with Nick. It was summertime again, and I had met him the previous summer. After just one more week of classes, I could work with Nick more.

We'll give it a break for the time being. Get into bed.

Even though it was early, he went to bed as ordered. He was too excited for one day and was in constant pain. Before long, sounds came from outside. "You have company, come into the living room," said Mom as she entered.

It was Mrs. Randall, Miss Jacobs, Miss Bruce, and Mr. Victor. "How are you feeling?" Mr. Victor enquired. We sincerely apologize for what transpired with you.

He answered, "I am fine other than the soreness from the punches."

"We want to thank you for what you did," Miss Bruce went on.

Startled, he asked, "Thank me?" He did not anticipate hearing that.

Yes, those boys have been bullying the teachers—including me—for a long time. They did not put forth the effort to earn their good grades. We were unable to confront their parents since they were too strong. I'm hoping you get it. We were, I suppose, simply cowards. Mrs. Randall had a genuine passion in her voice.

To him, confessing to a youngster was in any case abhorrent. It kind of stunned him. In response, Whitey said, "Yeah, I get it. Before I ever got to school, I was terrified of them. As you are aware, they had a reputation.

"You are bright, and we will look after you and your education," Miss Bruce went on. In any case, we will work to have you graduate right away. You know more about our subjects than we do, most teachers claim. We will be present at the board meeting to voice our opinions because we are all in agreement with the graduation.

Whitey had a grating way of bringing up the fact that the material a teacher was teaching did not always align with what was in the book. He would occasionally add that he didn't think the teacher or the book were correct. Naturally, The Boy would then weigh in on what he believed to be the correct idea. He would occasionally speak for ten minutes about a topic, which annoyed the other students and the teachers. Paradoxically, Whitey had made a self-promise to be silent in class this last year. Though he never finished the first day of the course, he did honor his promise.

"Wow, thank you is all I have to say." Although she had described him as intellectual, he was not in fact that manner. All he had to do was read a lot and remember what he had read.

Miss Bruce gave him a tight hug and walked away.

CHOICE AND BEING THE ONE: CHAPTER 3

The first step in finding the right relationship is to be very clear about what you want. It goes without saying that not everyone has the same goals in mind. Seeking a mate with similar relationship objectives is something you should do. While they don't have to be exactly on the same page, you should try to find someone who is at least in the same chapter as you. For instance, some people correspond online like pen pals for days or weeks at a time without ever meeting. Others only want to locate someone with whom they can hook up or have sex right away.

Despite the fact that nobody truly wants to remain with someone they are incompatible with, we frequently find ourselves in such situations. We frequently settle for subpar connections because we are hurrying through the most crucial periods and failing to see the clues that are there. Rather than waiting until the very end of the film to see if this individual is a perfect fit, why not take some time to find out? Before engaging in sexual activity, many of us have numerous things we'd like to know about our partner.

For instance, I'd like to know if a man can kiss well. Is he good enough at making out to not always need it to end in sex? Has the touch of him turned me on? Is he imaginative? Can he communicate his needs, wants, and wishes? Does he want to know about every aspect of my body, or just the more visible ones? Is he presentable? Does he have confidence? Does he have any fetishes that would be a turnoff? Long before I have sex with him, I would prefer to take the time to learn these things.

Have you ever been disappointed after going to bed with someone only to discover later that you were not compatible sexually and that, with a little more time, you could have avoided the awkwardness of the situation? How about doing some homework first? Exploration is the most important phase and may be a lot of fun! The basis for your romantic repertoire for the duration of your relationship is built by this stage-by-stage procedure. It enables you to create a highly rich, personal experience from the first kiss to the actual sexual encounter.

It makes sense why so many people rush into sexual relationships and why those relationships end so fast. By doing this, you enter a scenario knowing very little about the needs, desires, and wants of the other person. The majority of individuals will fall back on "the usual"—doing the same thing as everyone who has actually "came or not" before you. This isn't fancy sex. Because you two haven't had enough time to get to know one another well enough, you aren't being caressed and loved in a way that is exclusive to you. The idea is to have wonderful, powerful sex that is tailored just for the two of you.

Your partner's body and intellect are incredibly distinct from yours. Everybody reacts differently to various touch types, locations, settings, and other factors. Our tastes differ greatly from one another. Our habits and preferences are shaped by our past relationships and experiences. When you realize this, it becomes clear why going on multiple dates in between the initial kiss and sex is essential.

For some people, the idea of dedicating time to cultivate connection in this manner can be quite novel. You can still adhere to these rules, though, if you chose to have sex too young or if you're already married and want to rekindle your desire. You can begin to enjoy the advantages that will now become part of your knowledge base by getting back to the fundamentals and taking the time to invest in and repair your close connection.

A companion will open up to you both literally and figuratively once you make them feel comfortable. If the connection is intoxicating, they will also be more inclined to stick with it. If, after years of dating, they still act bashful or self-conscious around you, you should definitely consider starting over. Even in a committed relationship, things can still change. I can assure you that you may revive your dream of having a fantastic sexual life even if you have given up on it. You won't understand the amazing transformation that happens when you master the skill of passionate unfolding if you always follow the same routine.

While exploring the Million Things is immensely essential, you shouldn't approach it with the mindset that "I have all the time in the world." Sincerely, squandering time on the wrong person is just that—a waste. I hear comments like "nobody's perfect" and "I've been dating for years, so maybe this one is good enough" all the time from people. Could you please tell me when someone applied to be your Mr. or Ms. "Good Enough"? If someone had that kind of thought about you, how would you feel? Not to be offended and a little taken advantage of? I'll wager that you would rather they simply moved on to someone else if the roles were reversed. Alternatively, some people only stay with their partners for the sex. It's possible that they're not taking you out, hanging out with you, or introducing you to their loved ones. Though it hurts to say, you are being taken advantage of. It is easy for a week to grow into a month, and for a few months to turn into a year. Even though you could feel "comfortable," have you forgotten what kind of relationship you really wanted? Is remaining in a lousy relationship your justification for feeling "comfortable"?

The feeling of pursuing someone who isn't interested in you is something that everyone can understand. Individuals frequently subject each other to abuse even though no one should voluntarily agree to such. It's time to accept our own value and set higher standards for ourselves. Rather than compromising our dignity, let's begin establishing limits. How can you possibly make sense of spending weeks with an unexceptional match if your true objective is an outstanding relationship? When you can live a life full of passion, excitement, and remarkable relationships, why settle for ordinary?

"How many six months do you have?" posed a rhetorical question to me once by a friend. Consider how much time you have wasted looking for "the one," entering into relationships too soon, remaining in them after knowing they should end, ending or divorcing, grieving the loss of a relationship, and then beginning anew. It truly gets you to think about how much time you could have saved if you had gone on a few more dates to make sure you were with the right person in the first place.

You will spend a lot less time on the wrong ones, I can assure you, but I cannot guarantee that you will find the right one any faster. Many would contend—and I would agree—that even a failed relationship can teach us valuable lessons. But in my opinion, a wonderful relationship may also present a more remarkable chance for personal development. When two people approach a possible relationship with maturity and a shared desire to be open, inquisitive, and imaginative, you give each other a chance to grow and experience something you may never have had before.

How many of us can honestly claim to have had numerous exceptional relationships during our dating years? If we did, we would be less likely to be reading self-help books and more likely to be currently exploring an intimate, passionate and fulfilling relationship. There are a few things to start thinking about if you've reached the point where you find the thought of developing your relationships further intriguing. The first question to ask your self is, "What am I looking for?" You owe it to yourself and everyone you meet to be upfront about who you are and what you are looking for.

The most desirable traits in a companion ought to be those that you possess yourself. If you are looking for someone who is confident, happy, fiscally responsible, passionate, honest, communicative, emotionally and psychologically stable you must ask yourself if you are also those things. If you are looking for a woman or a man with certain physical traits, accept that you will probably attract people that are similarly driven. If your dream man must be tall, broad shouldered, athletic, with hair on his head but no facial or body hair, you must assume that men might have their own list of specific body traits for their ideal woman. Perhaps the guys that fit your specifications are looking for the "California look." They might want a blonde with long, straight hair, tanned, blue eyes that is no taller than 5'6". You can easily see how shortsighted this is.

With a cocky tone, Joey added, "Shit, didn't think I could do that."

Brenn attempted to concentrate on him, but his thoughts had dispersed and his body teetered on the verge of an orgasm. He managed to say, "Do what?" as Joey carelessly kissed and gently licked the top of his prick.

"Take that amount. I can absolutely take it in my ass if I can take nine inches in my mouth. Brenn was happy for Joey since it seemed like he was doing well, even though he was sad that Joey had stopped.

Is that correct? Joey enquired.

Brenn gave a nod. He was so close to shooting his load down Joey's throat, he just didn't have the courage to admit it. Nevertheless, Joey sent him a look that could only be described as menacing, put the tip back in his mouth, and began to suck further and deeper. Though not as deep as previously, it was still sufficient to almost bring Brenn back.

"Joey."

With a smile on his face, Joey continued to suck and tease the delicate skin under the crown with his tongue. When Joey took Brenn down his throat for the first time, it was clear that he knew what he was doing and that Brenn was going to come. Brenn had to accept that Joey was in charge and always has been. If Brenn wanted to regain control over their relationship, he had to act quickly or else he would always be at Joey's mercy. He wavered between doing what he thought was right and giving in to Joey's demands, finally conceding in silence that Joey would always have his way. As he was sure he would, he caved and moaned in surrender as Joey lapped up to his cock's sensitized head.

Joey licked Brenn's balls with one hand pressed on his stomach and then dragged one into a ready mouth. Brenn groaned, his body tensed, it was sweet torture. Brenn wasn't startled when Joey started to descend lower, encouraging him to stretch his legs wider and slip down on the chair since he knew, when his ball was released, that Joey was done with him. Brenn obliged because it would have been fatal for him to disobey.

He let out a gasp and trembled while Joey licked the opening of his body. His skin was teased by the smooth, slow, gentle strokes, and the constant focus caused his tight hole, which was seldom opened, to widen.

Biting his lip, Brenn closed his eyes and was acutely aware of his fingers pressing on the chair's arms. Joey pressed harder, and he shuddered once more.

Joey, that's great, by God. Brenn was compelled to encourage Joey even though she most likely didn't need it. He also couldn't resist spreading his legs apart and grabbing for his cock to give it a few firm pulls.

"Hey, mine!" Brenn was shocked by Joey's complaint and halted.

"I must come," he groaned. And that was putting it mildly. His cock felt like it was about to explode, and his balls were hurting so much that he had to come.

"Avoid touching. Not quite yet.

Joey, please. Brenn detested having to beg, but he was going crazy watching Joey treat him like this. He had never experienced love or the strong attraction to another person that could melt him the way Joey could. Everything became more personal and intense as a result. Brenn was drawn into a web of sensuous desire that was beyond anything he had ever experienced with each caress. It increased his awareness and sensitivity to the point where he felt as though the world was about to blow up. He sighed, thinking of how much better everything would be if Joey returned his affection.

"Not just yet." Brenn's expression said everything Joey needed to know, so she didn't even need to ask.

Brenn gave in, trying to calm himself down, not knowing if he could take much more. Joey resumed his tormenting him, gently caressing his nut sac with gentle yet firm lips, sucking in one testicle at a time. Brenn sighed with relief when Joey returned to his cock at last. When Joey sucked on him once more, he knew it would be the last time, and it wouldn't come any sooner.

Brenn, I'm about to blow you off. I'm going to push you really hard.

Joey stuck a finger in his mouth and pulled it out, dripping wet with saliva, while Brenn watched. Joey stared at Brenn with a blue glare that held him captive while he gently and carefully slipped his finger inside his ass.

"Oh my god!"

Joey pushed deeper and murmured, "Take it for me," immediately looking for the sweet spot that Brenn knew would make him scream when it arrived. That's all, Brenn. I want you to experience this and understand what it's like.

"Oh God, God Almighty!" Brenn scrambled under Joey's assault, skewering himself on Joey's finger and screamed as it touched the raw nerves that shot a bolt of lightning to his cock and lit a fire in his belly.

"You believe you're so strong and in charge, Brenn? You're going to lose your mind around me. Joey's tongue ran over the taut flesh behind Brenn's balls, punctuating his words. It was very excessive.

"Joey, I plan to attend!"

You're damn right, dude. In one swift motion, Joey leaned in and rimmed Brenn's pulsing shaft's head.

Joey's mouth sucked incessantly, hot and wet. Brenn was unable to wait. With a cry on his lips and his body bent from the power of the strongest orgasm he had ever experienced, he arrived as he had predicted.

Judging from the sight in his eyes, Joey swallowed every drop of cum, unrepentant and completely in love with it. Brenn observed with fascination as Joey thoroughly cleaned his penis and proceeded to give it another small suck just to be sure.

Brenn touched Joey's hair, hardly able to breathe normally again. "Do you enjoy eating cock, or is there something for which I am truly thankful?" Brenn inquired.

"I enjoy consuming yours. Unlike some others, you remain motionless and don't try to force it down my throat. It required several moments for Brenn to comprehend Joey's words due to his casual tone.

"Have other men injured you?" he inquired, becoming enraged at the idea that someone would harm Joey in that way.

Joey smiled after giving a shrug. "My teeth are here. They stop quickly enough.

Brenn recalled how Joey had gripped him tightly with his fangs, but it was only done to prevent Brenn from escaping. It didn't take him long to realize that would also be useful in the event that Joey was forced to do something against her will.

As Joey slid back onto Brenn's lap, Brenn automatically encircled him with his arms. Sensing the nervous strain in Joey's body, he questioned, "Do you want to come?"

"It's probably too soon, but I don't think it will work again, love to."

Section Three

Eva will visit six guys this year, including James. James is the seventeenth guy she has dated out of sixteen. He is a seventeen-year-old college student without ambition who is a touch spoiled for his age. He spends his mornings lounging around, not attending the college's early classes. He hangs out in bars with his pals in the evenings.

He fits in well with all the girls because of his amazing sense of humor, blonde hair, and blue eyes. It was only a coincidence that I ran into Eva in the grocery store. He's not the kind of responsible guy who shops for his house. He was in the grocery store, doing a mission set forth by his wealthy friend Dan: he needed to earn $100 to set up a date with a female he saw there. James had Eva, a beauty bumper for his challenge, money, and a fantastic female for the date, so it was an easy task.

"Will I ever find nice clothes to wear?" Eva mutters to herself as she looks through her closet for a suitable evening gown. Her parents have left for work, so she is by herself at home.

She finally gave up on having a room to herself with a separate staircase from the door to her room, giving her a sense of independence while yet allowing her parents to see her occasionally, after a considerable amount of aggravation with them.

Eva gets ready for the date while sporting a white bardot dress and a corset belt. This time, I'll go out first, hang out with James for a while, and only then—if I still feel the same way—may we end with a kiss. I ought to think about what Ana stated. She's not wrong. It won't hurt to go out with the guy. In order to find out if he is the one she is seeking for, Eva chooses to go out first and decides not to kiss.

Just in time to pick Eva up, James gives her a quick peck on the cheeks. His kind demeanor makes her feel like a princess. The way he holds the door for her, strokes her cheeks, and tucks her hair behind her ear when a tangle falls on her face impresses Eva.

When they could merely stroll to the cafe, Eva finds it unusual to get into his yellow Beetle. Her house is right around the corner from the Bistro eatery.

Breaking the stillness, Eva replies, "We could have just walked."

"We don't stroll. We take our car to the cafe. James grinned. "Wrong joke. Yes, we had the option. says James.

"But here we are now." James casts a glance outside. They've arrived at the cafe. "Perhaps we should take a quick drive later. That sounds like a really good concept to me. Say what?

"We'll see." Eva smiles back.

James approaches her and throws open the door.

"Oh, James, you don't have to. I am able to open the door by myself. It cheers Eva to see James taking care of her. Are these folks made anymore? Eva, a hopeless romantic, is moved by James's small acts of kindness.

They take a seat at a corner table with two chairs in the peaceful cafe Bistro, which is lit by a gentle yellow light.

"You look amazing in this dress," James remarks, giving Eva a warm glance.

"I'm grateful." Eva is overjoyed to learn this. Who enjoys receiving compliments? She gives a smile.

"So, Eva, how are you doing?" James looks into her eyes and asks.

Alright.And you?

"Very good, since I'm with you." James flashes his dimples when he smiles. He strokes his shiny hair with his hand.

"What are your preferences?" James queries.

Eva looks over the menu.

"Bruschetta?" Eva advises perusing the menu.

"And a little vino?Tempranillo, please.James queries.

"That sounds fantastic." Closing the menu card, Eva leaves it open on the table.

James places a wine and bruschetta order. He then directs his gaze to Eva. They discuss about pals, activities, and likes and dislikes.

"I enjoy going on hikes."

"Me too. I think we ought to go trekking sometime. James has thoughtful eyes that sparkle.

Who is your best friend, then?

"Ana. She is really adorable.

James makes her laugh with his charming one-liners, and they enjoy each other's company.

"What keeps you from having a boyfriend?" James drinks a wine and asks.

Eva doesn't say anything. Is he going to get it? Should I let him know? For Eva, everything appears to be in order. However, she follows her gut and withholds the whole reason from him.

It's not as though I was without a partner. Simply put, I don't have any at the moment. Eva informs James. How about you? You seem like a really kind person. How do you feel about being alone?

"Just like you're not dating at the moment." James smiles like the devil. Eva thinks there might be a problem with James because she finds his grins a little strange. Gives him the benefit of the doubt, though. I've judged him too much. He has a beautiful appearance. We share many similarities.

Eva considers abandoning the plan to kiss James and find out since, at this point, she is scared that James won't be what she wants when they share a kiss. She is terrified because she is so close to getting the ideal kiss. Or perhaps he's not the one? And she is struck down by the acrid, nasty memories of her previous numerous Fridays. She fears being alone forever, losing the opportunity to do something again, and her destiny.

When it's time to move, she observes Professor Mike eating dinner by himself across the table. She has no idea how long he has been sitting there, if he has seen her, or even whether he has heard her talking to James. Her cheeks flush. Why am I thinking about everyone all the time? Eva gives herself a curse and gets up to go with James.